In case of loss

_____

_____

_____

_____

As a reward: $ _____

Published by Moleskine SpA

Design and concept
Moleskine

Content consultant
Andrea Turco

ISBN 9788866131595

Manufactured in China

Download page templates and find translations
in a range of different languages at *moleskine.com/templates*
Key in on screen and/or write by hand.

1- Download   2- Print   3- Paste

CONTENTS

Downloadable Coaster Design Tool

9x9 cm

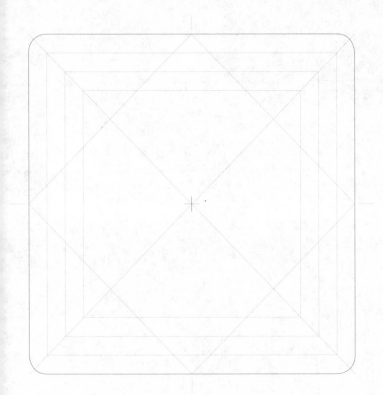

9x9 cm

Wish List

name · info	notes

name · info	notes	
		○
		○
		○
		○
		○
		○
		○
		○
		○
		○
		○
		○
		○
		○
		○
		○
		○
		○
		○
		○

Glossary

ABV *(Alcohol By Volume)*	Measure of how much alcohol is contained in a liquid, expressed as a percentage of total volume.
AG *(All Grain)*	Homebrewing technique using malt grain rather than malt extract.
Ale	Type of beer brewed using top fermentation.
Aroma Hop	Hop used to enhance the aroma of the beer.
Beer	Alcoholic beverage produced by the fermentation of malted barley and other cereals, usually flavoured with hops.
Biergarten	Open-air area in which food and beer are served, originating in Germany, particularly Bavaria.
Bittering Hop	Hop used to give a bitter flavour to the beer.
Blend	Mixture of different types of beers of variable percentages.
Boiling	Phase of brewing in which the wort is sterilized and some chemical processes occur.
Bottom Fermentation	Fermentation through the action of a particular type of yeast, *Saccharomyces Carlsbergensis*, at a temperature of between 6 and 12 °C; the yeast, at the end of this process, settles at the bottom.
Brettanomyces	Particular kind of yeast usually considered as a contaminant in brewing, but typical in some traditional types of beer.
Brewpub	Pub which brews and serves its own beer.
CAMRA *(Campaign for Real Ale)*	British consumer organization whose main aim is promoting traditional Anglo-Saxon beer (the organization has coined the name *Real Ale* for this type of beer) and the interests of local brewers and traditional British pubs.
Capping Machine	Machine used to cork bottles.
Carbonade Flamande	Traditional Belgian recipe, a sweet and sour beef stew braised in beer and seasoned with spices.
Carbonation	Process of carbon-dioxide formation in the beer which makes it fizzy, achieved either by adding sugars or fresh yeast before bottling or kegging (natural carbonation) or by direct injection of carbon dioxide (forced carbonation).
Cask	Traditional English container from which the beer is served without additional carbon-dioxide pressure.

Celis, Pierre Belgian brewer who opened his first brewery in 1966, so reviving the traditional blanche beer style.

Dry Hopping Technique of brewing based on the addition of dry hops: the hops are added at the end of the primary fermentation process rather than during boiling, in order to produce a very deep aroma and smell.

E+G
(Extract + Grains) Homebrewing technique in which the brewer uses a no-hop malt extract, hops and, usually, special grains.

EBC
(European Brewing Convention) Internationally used measuring system to specify the intensity of beer colour.

Ethanol Fermentation Process in which, by the action of appropriate yeasts, the greater part of sugars in the wort are converted into alcohol and carbon dioxide.

Fermentation Lock Valve used to release carbon dioxide created during alcoholic fermentation which, at the same time, prevents air from entering.

FG
(Final Gravity) Specific gravity of the wort measured at the end of fermentation.

Filtration Step after mashing in which the wort is filtered to remove spent grains.

Foam Layer of gas bubbles on the top of the beer formed, when pouring the beer, after the dispersion of carbon dioxide contained in it.

Gambrinus Legendary king of Flanders, known as the patron saint of beer and brewers.

Great British Beer Festival One of the most important beer exhibitions in the world which takes place in London every year. Focusing mainly on Anglo-Saxon products, it also includes selected foreign beers.

Groll, Josef Bavarian brewer who, in 1842 in the Czech Republic, developed the pilsner beer, one of the most influential and revolutionary styles in beer history.

Homebrewing Brewing on a domestic level.

Hop Creeping herbaceous plant. The brewing process uses its female flower clusters.

Hoppy Hop addition to the wort during boiling.

Hydrometer Instrument used to measure the density of liquids (the ratio of mass to volume).

IBU
(International Bitterness Unit) — Measuring system used to specify the bitterness of the beer.

Jackson, Michael — English writer and journalist, also known as "The Beer Hunter", who was one of the most important popularizers of beer culture.

Keg — Cylindrical container used to store, transport and serve beer.

Lactobacillus — Bacteria sometimes used in the brewing process.

Lager — Type of beer brewed using bottom fermentation.

Light-struck — The unpleasant aromas caused when a beer has been exposed to ultraviolet light for a long time.

Lovibond Degrees — Measuring system used to specify both the intensity of malt colour and, before the introduction of the SRM, the intensity of beer colour.

Malt — Grains of barley (or other cereals) that have been submitted to the malting process.

Malting — Process in which grains of barley (or other cereals) germinate and are then dried at the appropriate temperature.

Mashing — Mixing of the milled grain with hot water. This process activates the enzymes contained in the cereal, so that the malt turns into wort.

Milling — The cracking of the barley malt (or other malted cereal) in preparation for the brewing process.

OG
(Original Gravity) — Specific gravity of the wort measured before the beginning of fermentation.

Oktoberfest — The world's largest beer festival, which takes place every year in Munich, Bavaria, from late September to the beginning of October. Only six breweries are allowed to sell beer during this festival.

Pasteurization — Sterilization of the beer through heat.

Plato Degrees — Measuring system used to specify the sugar concentration in wort.

Priming — Addition of sugars or fresh yeast to the beer before bottling or kegging which activates refermentation.

Pub — Stands for Public House, a public place of Anglo-Saxon origin in which alcoholic beverages are served.

Refermentation — Reactivation of the yeast due to the addition of sugars or fresh yeast before bottling or kegging the beer; the refermentation leads to (natural) carbonation of the beer.

Reinheitsgebot	German law promulgated in 1516 in order to regulate beer production, first in Bavaria and then throughout Germany.
Saccharomyces Carlsbergensis	Type of yeast used for producing bottom-fermented beers. It was first isolated in Carlsberg's laboratories.
Saccharomyces Cerevisiae	Type of yeast used for producing top-fermented beers, bread and wine.
Sediment	Residue at the bottom of the bottle left by solid particles suspended in the liquid (usually yeast used for refermentation).
SG *(Specific Gravity)*	Ratio of the density of beer to the density of water.
Spent Grains	Insoluble elements of the malt remaining after the wort has been filtered.
Spontaneous Fermentation	Fermentation activated by wild yeast (i.e. natural yeast) with no help from the brewer.
SRM *(Standard Reference Method)*	Measuring system used in the USA to specify the intensity of beer colour.
St. Patrick's Day	Feast day celebrated on the 17th of March that commemorates Saint Patrick, patron saint of Ireland. For the occasion, many beer events – usually dedicated to stout beer – take place.
Top Fermentation	Fermentation through the action of a particular type of yeast, *Saccharomyces Cerevisiae*, at a temperature of between 15 and 25 °C; the yeast, at the end of this process, rises to the surface.
Trappist Beer	Beer produced by Trappist monks following specific criteria that allow it to be labelled *Authentic Trappist Product*. Today, only seven monasteries in the world are authorized to label their beer as Trappist beer.
Whirlpool Process	Circular moving of the wort used to remove impurities produced during boiling.
Yeast	Type of fungus of which more than 1,000 species have been identified. Some are used in bread production, some in the fermentation process of alcoholic beverages.

Glasses: Main Types

Pint Glass (Nonic Glass)

The most common Anglo-Saxon glass.
Its shape and the flare on the top
reduce foam formation on British ales
and enhance it on stout beers.
The American version is smaller.

Weißbierglas

Used for German wheat beers.
It has a lengthened shape that showcases
the foam and the appearance of the beer,
and flares at the top to enhance fruity
and spicy aromas.
Standard capacity: half a litre.

Snifter

Mainly used for Belgian strong ales.
Its hemispherical shape enhances
the volume of foam, while the wide
body allows the richness
of the aromas to stand out.

Balloon

Suitable for strong and intense beers
such as strong ale and barley wine.
Its special shape, almost a sphere, helps
concentrate the aromas, while the wide
body allows thermal exchange with the
environment, helping the beer to reach the
right tasting temperature in a short time.

Flute

An elegant glass for elegant
beers like Pils.
The long and narrow body enhances
the *perlage* (tiny bubbles), while
the stem prevents the overheating
of the beer caused
by heat from the hand.

Biconical Glass

Suitable for many types
of beers, it has a wide waist
and narrower mouth.
The use of this glass presumes
the *beheading* of the foam
on the top of it with a spatula.

Mug

Classic German glass, used especially
for Helles and Märzen.
The sturdy glass stops the beer
warming up quickly.
It comes in many sizes: the one-litre
glass is called a Maßkrug.

Kölschglass / Altglass

A slender cylinder.
The one for Kölsch holds 20 cl;
the one for Altbier,
slightly squatter, holds 30 cl.

Tulip

Perfect for aromatic
beers, particularly those
of Belgian inspiration.
The top of the glass widens out
a bit in order to help head retention,
and the wide body helps
to enhance the aromas.

Tumbler

A simple shape which was once
used for serving beers
to the working classes.
Today it is used for serving refreshing
Belgian Witbier and for particular
types of beers produced
by spontaneous fermentation.

Footed Glass

Used for elegant and clear beers
such as Pils and Helles.
Its narrow mouth promotes
foam formation and retention.

Footed Pilsner Glass

Suitable for different types
of beers, in particular for Pils.
Tall and slender, it promotes
generous foam formation
and showcases the appearance
of the beer.

Pouring Beer

The Standard Pour

Pouring is an essential part of the beer-tasting experience. These are the basic directions you should follow to pour most beers.

· *Take your bottle of beer and a proper glass (it is very important that your glass is perfectly clean) and then hold the glass at a 45-degree angle.*

· *Pour the beer steadily and confidently, aiming for the middle of the glass's side.*

· *When the glass is just over half full, tilt it back to an upright position and continue to pour. In this way you will get the proper amount of foam on top.*

The Bottle-Conditioned Pour

Unfiltered beers are called "bottle-conditioned beers" because they still contain active yeast so that the beer continues to ferment, mature and carbonate in the bottle.
With these you don't want to drink the sediment, which requires careful pouring.

· *Tilt the glass at a 45-degree angle and pour the beer into it slowly and gently.*

· *As before, when the glass is just over half full, tilt it back to an upright position and continue to pour. In this way you will get the proper amount of foam on top.*

· *Towards the end of the bottle, when you begin to get to the yeast (you'll see it turn cloudy), be careful not to pour it into the glass.*

· *Leave the rest of the beer in the bottle; the yeast is slightly unpalatable and can be heavy to digest.*

The Hefeweizen Pour

German wheat beers are also bottle-conditioned beers, but in this case, the focal point of their flavour is the yeast. When you pour these beers you actually want to pour out the yeast that tends to settle in the bottom of the bottle.

· *Try to use the correct glass, tall enough to accommodate plenty of foam, to avoid overflowing, because these beers are highly carbonated.*
As before, tilt the glass at a 45-degree angle and pour the beer into it particularly slowly and gently.

· *When the glass is just over half full, tilt it back to an upright position and continue to pour. In this way you will get the proper amount of foam on top.*

· *To make sure you pour all the contents of the bottle into your glass, leave a little beer in the bottle and swirl it gently so that the beer sediment is collected off the bottom.*

· *Pour the remaining beer into your glass.*

Useful Measures and Conversions

capacity

16 ounces = 1 U.S. pint
20 ounces = 1 imperial (UK) pint
2 cups = 1 pint
2 pints = 1 quart
4 quarts = 1 gallon
1.2009 U.S. gallons = 1 imperial (UK) gallon
10 ml = 1 cl
100 cl = 1 l
100 l = 1 hl
1 U.S. quart = 0.9464 l
1.0567 U.S. quarts = 1 l
1 U.S. gallon = 3.7854 l
0.2642 U.S. gallon = 1 l
1 imperial (UK) gallon = 4.5460 l
0.2200 imperial (UK) gallon = 1 l

°F	-40	-31	-22	-13	-4	5	14	23	32	41	50	59	68	77	86	95	104
°C	-40	-35	-30	-25	-20	-15	-10	-5	0	5	10	15	20	25	30	35	40

°F = (°C x 9/5)+32   °C = (°F -32) x 5/9

Beer Journal

beer

ABV

style

colour

○ draft
○ bottle
○ ...

producer

country · region

suggested glass

serving temperature

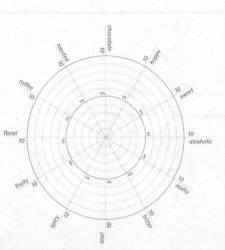

tasting

when

where

appearance

nose

taste

opinion · notes

chocolate
10
roasted
10
10 hoppy
toffee
10
10 sweet
5 *5*
5 *5*
floral
10
5 *5*
5
10 alcoholic
fruity *10*
5 *5*
5 *5*
10 malty
spicy *10*
10 bitter
sour *10*

rating ☆☆☆☆☆

beer

ABV

style

colour

○ draft
○ bottle
○ ...

producer

country · region

suggested glass

serving temperature

tasting

when

where

appearance

nose

taste

opinion · notes

rating ☆☆☆☆☆

beer

ABV

style

colour

○ draft
○ bottle
○ ...

producer

country · region

suggested glass

serving temperature

tasting

when

where

appearance

nose

taste

chocolate
10

roasted
10

toffee
10

5

5

5

10
hoppy

10
sweet

floral
10

5

5

5

10
alcoholic

fruity
10

5

5

5

10
malty

spicy
10

sour
10

10
bitter

opinion · notes

rating ☆☆☆☆☆

beer

ABV

style

colour

- ○ draft
- ○ bottle
- ○ ...

producer

country · region

suggested glass

serving temperature

tasting

when

where

appearance

nose

taste

opinion · notes

rating ☆☆☆☆☆

beer ABV

style colour

○ draft
○ bottle
○ ...

producer country · region

suggested glass serving temperature

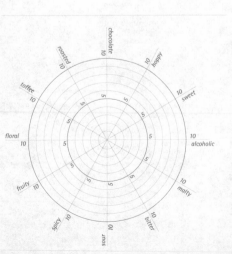

tasting

when

where

appearance

nose

taste

opinion · notes

rating ☆☆☆☆☆

beer

ABV

style

colour

○ draft
○ bottle
○ ...

producer

country · region

suggested glass

serving temperature

tasting

when

where

appearance

nose

taste

opinion · notes

rating ☆☆☆☆☆

beer		ABV

style	colour	○ draft
		○ bottle
		○ ...

producer	country · region

suggested glass

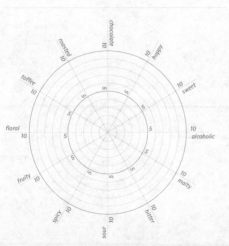

serving temperature

tasting

when

where

appearance

nose

taste

opinion · notes

rating ☆☆☆☆☆

beer

ABV

style

colour

○ draft
○ bottle
○ ...

producer

country · region

suggested glass

serving temperature

tasting

when

where

appearance

nose

taste

opinion · notes

rating ☆☆☆☆☆

beer	ABV

style	colour	○ draft
		○ bottle
		○ ...

producer	country · region

suggested glass 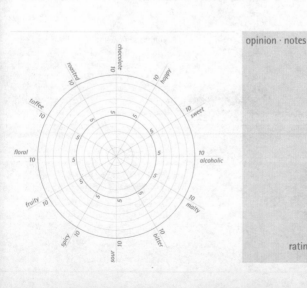 serving temperature

tasting

when

where

appearance

nose

taste

opinion · notes

rating ☆☆☆☆☆

beer

ABV

style

colour

○ draft
○ bottle
○ ...

producer

country · region

suggested glass

serving temperature

tasting

when

where

appearance

nose

taste

chocolate
10

roasted
10

hoppy
10

toffee
10

10
sweet

floral
10

5
5
5
5
5

10
alcoholic

fruity
10

10
malty

spicy
10

10
bitter

sour
10

opinion · notes

rating ☆☆☆☆☆

beer　　　　　　　　　　　　　　　　　　　　　　ABV

style　　　　　　　　　　　　　　colour　　　　　　○ draft
　　　　　　　　　　　　　　　　　　　　　　　　　○ bottle
　　　　　　　　　　　　　　　　　　　　　　　　　○ ...

producer　　　　　　　　　　　　country · region

suggested glass　　　　　　　　　　　　　　　　serving temperature

tasting
　　　　　　　　when

　　　　　　　where

appearance

nose

taste

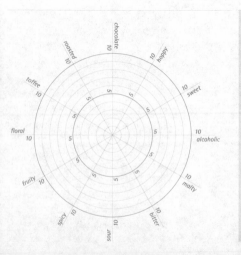

opinion · notes

rating ☆☆☆☆☆

beer

ABV

style

colour

○ draft
○ bottle
○ ...

producer

country · region

suggested glass

serving temperature

tasting

when

where

appearance

nose

taste

chocolate
10
roasted 10
hoppy 10
toffee 10
sweet 10
floral 10
alcoholic 10
fruity 10
malty 10
spicy 10
bitter 10
sour 10
5

opinion · notes

rating ☆☆☆☆☆

beer   ABV

style   colour   ○ draft
                                                                     ○ bottle
                                                                     ○ ...

producer   country · region

suggested glass   serving temperature

tasting
                    when

                    where

appearance

nose

taste

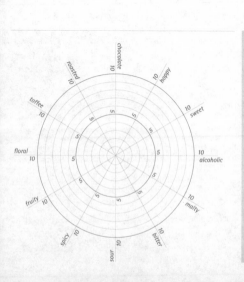

opinion · notes

rating ☆☆☆☆☆

beer

ABV

style

colour

○ draft
○ bottle
○ ...

producer

country · region

suggested glass

serving temperature

tasting

when

where

appearance

nose

taste

opinion · notes

rating ☆☆☆☆☆

beer

ABV

style

colour

○ draft
○ bottle
○ ...

producer

country · region

suggested glass

serving temperature

tasting

when

where

appearance

nose

taste

opinion · notes

rating ☆☆☆☆☆

beer

ABV

style

colour

○ draft
○ bottle
○ ...

producer

country · region

suggested glass

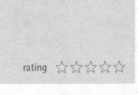

serving temperature

tasting

when

where

appearance

nose

taste

chocolate
10
roasted
10
hoppy
10
toffee
10
sweet
10
floral
10
alcoholic
10
fruity
10
malty
10
spicy
10
bitter
10
sour
10
5

opinion · notes

rating ☆☆☆☆☆

beer

ABV

style

colour

○ draft
○ bottle
○ ...

producer

country · region

suggested glass

serving temperature

tasting

when

where

appearance

nose

taste

chocolate
10
roasted 10
toffee 10
floral 10
fruity 10
spicy 10
sour 10
bitter 10
malty 10
alcoholic 10
sweet 10
hoppy 10
5

opinion · notes

rating ☆☆☆☆☆

beer

ABV

style

colour

○ draft
○ bottle
○ ...

producer

country · region

suggested glass

serving temperature

tasting

when

where

appearance

nose

taste

opinion · notes

rating ☆☆☆☆☆

beer		ABV

style	colour	○ draft
		○ bottle
		○ ...

producer	country · region

suggested glass

serving temperature

tasting

when

where

appearance

nose

taste

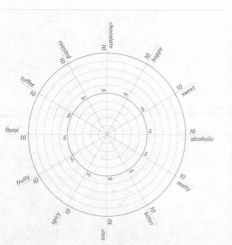

opinion · notes

rating ☆☆☆☆☆

beer	ABV

style	colour	○ draft
		○ bottle
		○ ...

producer	country · region

suggested glass

serving temperature

tasting

when

where

appearance

nose

taste

opinion · notes

rating ☆☆☆☆☆

beer

ABV

style

colour

○ draft
○ bottle
○ ...

producer

country · region

suggested glass

serving temperature

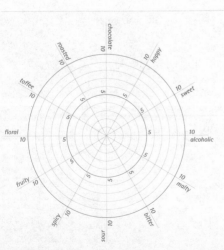

tasting

when

where

appearance

nose

taste

opinion · notes

rating ☆☆☆☆☆

beer

ABV

style

colour

○ draft
○ bottle
○ ...

producer

country · region

suggested glass

serving temperature

tasting

when

where

appearance

nose

taste

opinion · notes

rating ☆☆☆☆☆

beer

ABV

style

colour

○ draft
○ bottle
○ ...

producer

country · region

suggested glass

serving temperature

tasting

when

where

appearance

nose

taste

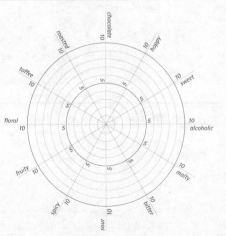

opinion · notes

rating ☆☆☆☆☆

41

beer

ABV

style

colour

○ draft
○ bottle
○ ...

producer

country · region

suggested glass

serving temperature

tasting

when

where

appearance

nose

taste

chocolate
10
roasted
10
hoppy
10
toffee
10
sweet
10
floral
10
alcoholic
10
5
5
5
5
5
5
5
5
fruity
10
malty
10
spicy
10
bitter
10
sour
10

opinion · notes

rating ☆☆☆☆☆

beer

ABV

style

colour

○ draft
○ bottle
○ ...

producer

country · region

suggested glass

serving temperature

tasting

when

where

appearance

nose

taste

opinion · notes

rating ☆☆☆☆☆

beer

ABV

style

colour

○ draft
○ bottle
○ ...

producer

country · region

suggested glass

serving temperature

tasting

when

where

appearance

nose

taste

opinion · notes

rating ☆☆☆☆☆

beer		ABV

style	colour	○ draft
		○ bottle
		○ ...

producer	country · region

suggested glass serving temperature

tasting

when

where

appearance

nose

taste

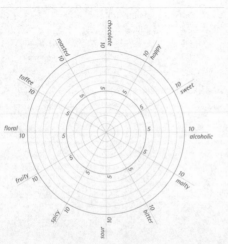

opinion · notes

rating ☆☆☆☆☆

beer

ABV

style

colour

○ draft
○ bottle
○ ...

producer

country · region

suggested glass

serving temperature

tasting

when

where

appearance

nose

taste

opinion · notes

rating ☆☆☆☆☆

beer		ABV

style	colour	○ draft
		○ bottle
		○ ...

producer	country · region

suggested glass   serving temperature

tasting

when

where

appearance

nose

taste

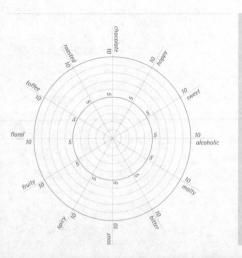

opinion · notes

rating ☆☆☆☆☆

beer

ABV

style

colour

○ draft
○ bottle
○ ...

producer

country · region

suggested glass

serving temperature

tasting

when

where

appearance

nose

taste

chocolate
10

roasted
10

hoppy
10

toffee
10

10 sweet

5

floral
10

5

10 alcoholic

fruity
10

10 malty

spicy
10

10 bitter

10 sour

opinion · notes

rating ☆☆☆☆☆

beer | ABV

style | colour | ○ draft
| | ○ bottle
| | ○ ...

producer | country · region

suggested glass | serving temperature

tasting

when

where

appearance

nose

taste

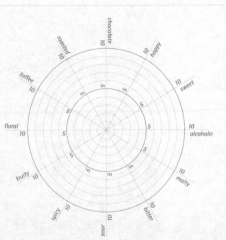

opinion · notes

rating ☆☆☆☆☆

beer

ABV

style

colour

○ draft
○ bottle
○ ...

producer

country · region

suggested glass

serving temperature

tasting

when

where

appearance

nose

taste

chocolate
10
roasted
10
hoppy
10
toffee
10
5
5
sweet
10
floral
10
5
5
alcoholic
10
fruity
10
5
5
malty
10
spicy
10
bitter
10
sour
10

opinion · notes

rating ☆☆☆☆☆

beer

ABV

style

colour

○ draft
○ bottle
○ ...

producer

country · region

suggested glass

serving temperature

tasting

when

where

appearance

nose

taste

chocolate
10

roasted
10

toffee
10

floral
10

fruity
10

spicy
10

sour
10

bitter
10

malty
10

alcoholic
10

sweet
10

hoppy
10

5

opinion · notes

rating ☆☆☆☆☆

beer

ABV

style

colour

○ draft
○ bottle
○ ...

producer

country · region

suggested glass

serving temperature

tasting

when

where

appearance

nose

taste

chocolate
10

roasted
10

happy
10

toffee
10

sweet
10

5

5

5

5

floral
10

5

5

alcoholic
10

5

5

fruity
10

malty
10

spicy
10

sour
10

bitter
10

opinion · notes

rating ☆☆☆☆☆

beer

ABV

style

colour

○ draft
○ bottle
○ ...

producer

country · region

suggested glass

serving temperature

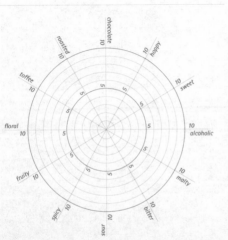

tasting

when

where

appearance

nose

taste

opinion · notes

chocolate
10

roasted
10

hoppy
10

toffee
10

10 sweet

5

5

5

5

5

5

5

5

floral
10

5

5

10
alcoholic

fruity
10

10
malty

spicy
10

10
bitter

sour
10

rating ☆☆☆☆☆

beer

ABV

style

colour

○ draft
○ bottle
○ ...

producer

country · region

suggested glass

serving temperature

tasting

when

where

appearance

nose

taste

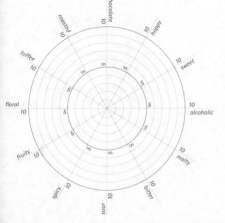

opinion · notes

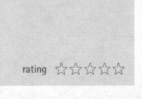

rating ☆☆☆☆☆

beer

ABV

style

colour

○ draft
○ bottle
○ ...

producer

country · region

suggested glass

serving temperature

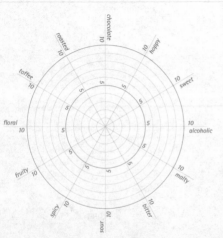

tasting

when

where

appearance

nose

taste

opinion · notes

chocolate
10

roasted
10

hoppy
10

toffee
10

sweet
10

floral
10

alcoholic
10

fruity
10

malty
10

spicy
10

bitter
10

sour
10

5

rating ☆☆☆☆☆

beer

ABV

style

colour

- ○ draft
- ○ bottle
- ○ ...

producer

country · region

suggested glass

serving temperature

tasting

when

where

appearance

nose

taste

opinion · notes

rating ☆☆☆☆☆

beer   ABV

style   colour   ○ draft
                                                                  ○ bottle
                                                                  ○ ...

producer   country · region

suggested glass   serving temperature

tasting
                    when

                    where

appearance

nose

taste

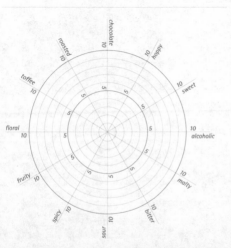

opinion · notes

rating ☆☆☆☆☆

beer

ABV

style

colour

○ draft
○ bottle
○ ...

producer

country · region

suggested glass

serving temperature

tasting

when

where

appearance

nose

taste

chocolate
10
roasted
10
hoppy
10
toffee
10
sweet
10
floral
10
alcoholic
10
fruity
10
malty
10
spicy
10
bitter
10
sour
10
5

opinion · notes

rating ☆☆☆☆☆

name	bought on	drunk on
producer	country	year
colour	style	
notes		

☆☆☆☆☆

name	bought on	drunk on
producer	country	year
colour	style	
notes		

☆☆☆☆☆

name	bought on	drunk on
producer	country	year
colour	style	
notes		

☆☆☆☆☆

name	bought on	drunk on
producer	country	year
colour	style	

notes

☆☆☆☆☆

name	bought on	drunk on
producer	country	year
colour	style	

notes

☆☆☆☆☆

name	bought on	drunk on
producer	country	year
colour	style	

notes

☆☆☆☆☆

name	bought on	drunk on
producer	country	year
colour	style	
notes		

☆☆☆☆☆

name	bought on	drunk on
producer	country	year
colour	style	
notes		

☆☆☆☆☆

name	bought on	drunk on
producer	country	year
colour	style	
notes		

☆☆☆☆☆

name

bought on

drunk on

producer

country

year

colour

style

notes

☆☆☆☆☆

name

bought on

drunk on

producer

country

year

colour

style

notes

☆☆☆☆☆

name

bought on

drunk on

producer

country

year

colour

style

notes

☆☆☆☆☆

name	bought on	drunk on
producer	country	year
colour	style	
notes		

☆ ☆ ☆ ☆ ☆

name	bought on	drunk on
producer	country	year
colour	style	
notes		

☆ ☆ ☆ ☆ ☆

name	bought on	drunk on
producer	country	year
colour	style	
notes		

☆ ☆ ☆ ☆ ☆

name	bought on	drunk on
producer	country	year
colour	style	
notes		

☆☆☆☆☆

name	bought on	drunk on
producer	country	year
colour	style	
notes		

☆☆☆☆☆

name	bought on	drunk on
producer	country	year
colour	style	
notes		

☆☆☆☆☆

name	bought on	drunk on
producer	country	year
colour	style	
notes		

☆☆☆☆☆

name	bought on	drunk on
producer	country	year
colour	style	
notes		

☆☆☆☆☆

name	bought on	drunk on
producer	country	year
colour	style	
notes		

☆☆☆☆☆

name

bought on

drunk on

producer

country

year

colour

style

notes

☆☆☆☆☆

name

bought on

drunk on

producer

country

year

colour

style

notes

☆☆☆☆☆

name

bought on

drunk on

producer

country

year

colour

style

notes

☆☆☆☆☆

name	bought on	drunk on
producer	country	year
colour	style	
notes		

☆☆☆☆☆

name	bought on	drunk on
producer	country	year
colour	style	
notes		

☆☆☆☆☆

name	bought on	drunk on
producer	country	year
colour	style	
notes		

☆☆☆☆☆

name	bought on	drunk on
producer	country	year
colour	style	
notes		

☆☆☆☆☆

name	bought on	drunk on
producer	country	year
colour	style	
notes		

☆☆☆☆☆

name	bought on	drunk on
producer	country	year
colour	style	
notes		

☆☆☆☆☆

name	bought on	drunk on
producer	country	year
colour	style	
notes		

☆☆☆☆☆

name	bought on	drunk on
producer	country	year
colour	style	
notes		

☆☆☆☆☆

name	bought on	drunk on
producer	country	year
colour	style	
notes		

☆☆☆☆☆

name

bought on

drunk on

producer

country

year

colour

style

notes

☆☆☆☆☆

name

bought on

drunk on

producer

country

year

colour

style

notes

☆☆☆☆☆

name

bought on

drunk on

producer

country

year

colour

style

notes

☆☆☆☆☆

name	bought on	drunk on
producer	country	year
colour	style	

notes

☆☆☆☆☆

name	bought on	drunk on
producer	country	year
colour	style	

notes

☆☆☆☆☆

name	bought on	drunk on
producer	country	year
colour	style	

notes

☆☆☆☆☆

name	bought on	drunk on
producer	country	year
colour	style	

notes

☆☆☆☆☆

name	bought on	drunk on
producer	country	year
colour	style	

notes

☆☆☆☆☆

name	bought on	drunk on
producer	country	year
colour	style	

notes

☆☆☆☆☆

74

name	bought on	drunk on
producer	country	year
colour	style	
notes		

☆☆☆☆☆

name	bought on	drunk on
producer	country	year
colour	style	
notes		

☆☆☆☆☆

name	bought on	drunk on
producer	country	year
colour	style	
notes		

☆☆☆☆☆

name

bought on

drunk on

producer

country

year

colour

style

notes

☆☆☆☆☆

name

bought on

drunk on

producer

country

year

colour

style

notes

☆☆☆☆☆

name

bought on

drunk on

producer

country

year

colour

style

notes

☆☆☆☆☆

name	bought on	drunk on
producer	country	year
colour	style	

notes

☆☆☆☆☆

name	bought on	drunk on
producer	country	year
colour	style	

notes

☆☆☆☆☆

name	bought on	drunk on
producer	country	year
colour	style	

notes

☆☆☆☆☆

name	bought on	drunk on
producer	country	year
colour	style	
notes		☆☆☆☆☆

name	bought on	drunk on
producer	country	year
colour	style	
notes		☆☆☆☆☆

name	bought on	drunk on
producer	country	year
colour	style	
notes		☆☆☆☆☆

name	bought on	drunk on
producer	country	year
colour	style	
notes		

☆☆☆☆☆

name	bought on	drunk on
producer	country	year
colour	style	
notes		

☆☆☆☆☆

name	bought on	drunk on
producer	country	year
colour	style	
notes		

☆☆☆☆☆

name

bought on

drunk on

producer

country

year

colour

style

notes

☆ ☆ ☆ ☆ ☆

name

bought on

drunk on

producer

country

year

colour

style

notes

☆ ☆ ☆ ☆ ☆

name

bought on

drunk on

producer

country

year

colour

style

notes

☆ ☆ ☆ ☆ ☆

difficulty

○ ○ ○ ○ ○

recipe

serves

② ④ ⑥ ⑧ ⋯

ingredients

beer

preparation time

cooking time

cooking process

preparation

pairings

notes

rating

☆ ☆ ☆ ☆ ☆

recipe

difficulty

○ ○ ○ ○ ○

ingredients

serves

② ④ ⑥ ⑧ ⋯

beer

preparation time

cooking time

cooking process

pairings

preparation

notes

rating

☆ ☆ ☆ ☆ ☆

difficulty

recipe

○ ○ ○ ○ ○

serves

ingredients

② ④ ⑥ ⑧ …

beer

preparation time

cooking time

cooking process

preparation

pairings

notes

rating

☆ ☆ ☆ ☆ ☆

recipe

difficulty

○ ○ ○ ○ ○

ingredients

serves

② ④ ⑥ ⑧ ⋯

beer

preparation time

cooking time

cooking process

pairings

preparation

notes

rating

☆ ☆ ☆ ☆ ☆

difficulty

○ ○ ○ ○ ○

recipe

serves

② ④ ⑥ ⑧ ⋯

ingredients

beer

preparation time

cooking time

cooking process

pairings

preparation

notes

rating

☆☆☆☆☆

recipe

difficulty

○ ○ ○ ○ ○

ingredients

beer

serves

② ④ ⑥ ⑧ ⋯

preparation time

cooking time

cooking process

pairings

preparation

notes

rating

☆ ☆ ☆ ☆ ☆

difficulty

recipe

○ ○ ○ ○ ○

serves

ingredients

② ④ ⑥ ⑧ ⋯

beer

preparation time

cooking time

cooking process

preparation

pairings

notes

rating

☆ ☆ ☆ ☆ ☆

recipe

difficulty

○ ○ ○ ○ ○

ingredients

serves

② ④ ⑥ ⑧ ⋯

beer

preparation time

cooking time

cooking process

pairings

preparation

notes

rating

☆ ☆ ☆ ☆ ☆

difficulty

recipe

○ ○ ○ ○ ○

serves

ingredients

② ④ ⑥ ⑧ ⋯

beer

preparation time

cooking time

cooking process

pairings

notes

preparation

rating

☆ ☆ ☆ ☆ ☆

recipe

difficulty

○ ○ ○ ○ ○

ingredients

beer

serves

② ④ ⑥ ⑧ ⋯

preparation time

cooking time

cooking process

pairings

preparation

notes

rating

☆ ☆ ☆ ☆ ☆

difficulty

○ ○ ○ ○ ○

recipe

serves

② ④ ⑥ ⑧ ⋯

ingredients

beer

preparation time

cooking time

cooking process

pairings

preparation

notes

rating

☆ ☆ ☆ ☆ ☆

recipe

difficulty

○ ○ ○ ○ ○

ingredients

serves

② ④ ⑥ ⑧ ⋯

beer

preparation time

cooking time

cooking process

pairings

preparation

notes

rating

☆ ☆ ☆ ☆ ☆

difficulty

○ ○ ○ ○ ○

recipe

serves

② ④ ⑥ ⑧ ⋯

ingredients

beer

preparation time

cooking time

cooking process

pairings

notes

rating

☆ ☆ ☆ ☆ ☆

preparation

recipe

difficulty

○ ○ ○ ○ ○

ingredients

serves

② ④ ⑥ ⑧ ⋯

beer

preparation time

cooking time

cooking process

pairings

preparation

notes

rating

☆ ☆ ☆ ☆ ☆

difficulty

○ ○ ○ ○ ○

recipe

serves

② ④ ⑥ ⑧ ⋯

ingredients

beer

preparation time

cooking time

cooking process

pairings

preparation

notes

rating

☆ ☆ ☆ ☆ ☆

recipe

difficulty

○ ○ ○ ○ ○

ingredients

beer

serves

② ④ ⑥ ⑧ ⋯

preparation time

cooking time

cooking process

pairings

preparation

notes

rating

☆ ☆ ☆ ☆ ☆

difficulty

recipe

○ ○ ○ ○ ○

serves

ingredients

② ④ ⑥ ⑧ ⋯

beer

preparation time

cooking time

cooking process

preparation

pairings

notes

rating

☆ ☆ ☆ ☆ ☆

recipe

difficulty

○ ○ ○ ○ ○

ingredients

serves

② ④ ⑥ ⑧ ⋯

beer

preparation time

cooking time

cooking process

pairings

preparation

notes

rating

☆ ☆ ☆ ☆ ☆

difficulty

○ ○ ○ ○ ○

recipe

serves

② ④ ⑥ ⑧ ⋯

ingredients

beer

preparation time

cooking time

cooking process

pairings

notes

preparation

rating

☆ ☆ ☆ ☆ ☆

recipe

ingredients

beer

preparation

difficulty

○ ○ ○ ○ ○

serves

② ④ ⑥ ⑧ …

preparation time

cooking time

cooking process

pairings

notes

rating

☆ ☆ ☆ ☆ ☆

difficulty

○ ○ ○ ○ ○

recipe

serves

② ④ ⑥ ⑧ ⋯

ingredients

beer

preparation time

cooking time

cooking process

pairings

preparation

notes

rating

☆ ☆ ☆ ☆ ☆

recipe

difficulty

○ ○ ○ ○ ○

ingredients

serves

② ④ ⑥ ⑧ ⋯

beer

preparation time

cooking time

cooking process

preparation

pairings

notes

rating

☆ ☆ ☆ ☆ ☆

difficulty

○ ○ ○ ○ ○

recipe

serves

② ④ ⑥ ⑧ ⋯

ingredients

beer

preparation time

cooking time

cooking process

pairings

preparation

notes

rating

☆ ☆ ☆ ☆ ☆

recipe

difficulty

○ ○ ○ ○ ○

ingredients

serves

② ④ ⑥ ⑧ ⋯

beer

preparation time

cooking time

cooking process

pairings

preparation

notes

rating

☆ ☆ ☆ ☆ ☆

difficulty

recipe

○ ○ ○ ○ ○

serves

ingredients

② ④ ⑥ ⑧ ⋯

beer

preparation time

cooking time

cooking process

preparation

pairings

notes

rating

☆ ☆ ☆ ☆ ☆

recipe

difficulty

○ ○ ○ ○ ○

ingredients

serves

② ④ ⑥ ⑧ ⋯

beer

preparation time

cooking time

cooking process

pairings

preparation

notes

rating

☆ ☆ ☆ ☆ ☆

difficulty

recipe

○ ○ ○ ○ ○

serves

ingredients

② ④ ⑥ ⑧ ⋯

beer

preparation time

cooking time

cooking process

preparation

pairings

notes

rating

☆ ☆ ☆ ☆ ☆

recipe

difficulty

○ ○ ○ ○ ○

ingredients

beer

serves

② ④ ⑥ ⑧ ⋯

preparation time

cooking time

cooking process

pairings

preparation

notes

rating

☆ ☆ ☆ ☆ ☆

difficulty

recipe

○ ○ ○ ○ ○

serves

ingredients

② ④ ⑥ ⑧ ⋯

beer

preparation time

cooking time

cooking process

preparation

pairings

notes

rating

☆ ☆ ☆ ☆ ☆

recipe

difficulty

○ ○ ○ ○ ○

ingredients

serves

② ④ ⑥ ⑧ ⋯

beer

preparation time

cooking time

cooking process

pairings

preparation

notes

rating

☆ ☆ ☆ ☆ ☆

My Addresses

name

address · phone · website   opening hours

beers served / sold

my favourite beer   notes

name

address · phone · website   opening hours

beers served / sold

my favourite beer   notes

name

address · phone · website   opening hours

beers served / sold

my favourite beer   notes

name

address · phone · website

opening hours

beers served / sold

my favourite beer

notes

name

address · phone · website

opening hours

beers served / sold

my favourite beer

notes

name

address · phone · website

opening hours

beers served / sold

my favourite beer

notes

name

address · phone · website   opening hours

beers served / sold

my favourite beer   notes

name

address · phone · website   opening hours

beers served / sold

my favourite beer   notes

name

address · phone · website   opening hours

beers served / sold

my favourite beer   notes

name

address · phone · website

opening hours

beers served / sold

my favourite beer

notes

name

address · phone · website

opening hours

beers served / sold

my favourite beer

notes

name

address · phone · website

opening hours

beers served / sold

my favourite beer

notes

name

address · phone · website

opening hours

beers served / sold

my favourite beer

notes

name

address · phone · website

opening hours

beers served / sold

my favourite beer

notes

name

address · phone · website

opening hours

beers served / sold

my favourite beer

notes

name

address · phone · website

opening hours

beers served / sold

my favourite beer

notes

name

address · phone · website

opening hours

beers served / sold

my favourite beer

notes

name

address · phone · website

opening hours

beers served / sold

my favourite beer

notes

name

address · phone · website

opening hours

beers served / sold

my favourite beer

notes

name

address · phone · website

opening hours

beers served / sold

my favourite beer

notes

name

address · phone · website

opening hours

beers served / sold

my favourite beer

notes

name

address · phone · website   opening hours

beers served / sold

my favourite beer   notes

name

address · phone · website   opening hours

beers served / sold

my favourite beer   notes

name

address · phone · website   opening hours

beers served / sold

my favourite beer   notes

name

address · phone · website   opening hours

beers served / sold

my favourite beer   notes

name

address · phone · website   opening hours

beers served / sold

my favourite beer   notes

name

address · phone · website   opening hours

beers served / sold

my favourite beer   notes

name

address · phone · website   opening hours

beers served / sold

my favourite beer   notes

name

address · phone · website   opening hours

beers served / sold

my favourite beer   notes

name

address · phone · website   opening hours

beers served / sold

my favourite beer   notes

name

address · phone · website   opening hours

beers served / sold

my favourite beer   notes

name

address · phone · website   opening hours

beers served / sold

my favourite beer   notes

name

address · phone · website   opening hours

beers served / sold

my favourite beer   notes

name

address · phone · website   opening hours

beers served / sold

my favourite beer   notes

name

address · phone · website   opening hours

beers served / sold

my favourite beer   notes

name

address · phone · website   opening hours

beers served / sold

my favourite beer   notes

name

address · phone · website   opening hours

beers served / sold

my favourite beer   notes

name

address · phone · website   opening hours

beers served / sold

my favourite beer   notes

name

address · phone · website   opening hours

beers served / sold

my favourite beer   notes

name

address · phone · website   opening hours

beers served / sold

my favourite beer   notes

name

address · phone · website   opening hours

beers served / sold

my favourite beer   notes

name

address · phone · website   opening hours

beers served / sold

my favourite beer   notes

name

address · phone · website · opening hours

beers served / sold

my favourite beer · notes

name

address · phone · website · opening hours

beers served / sold

my favourite beer · notes

name

address · phone · website · opening hours

beers served / sold

my favourite beer · notes

name

address · phone · website

opening hours

beers served / sold

my favourite beer

notes

name

address · phone · website

opening hours

beers served / sold

my favourite beer

notes

name

address · phone · website

opening hours

beers served / sold

my favourite beer

notes

name

address · phone · website   opening hours

beers served / sold

my favourite beer   notes

name

address · phone · website   opening hours

beers served / sold

my favourite beer   notes

name

address · phone · website   opening hours

beers served / sold

my favourite beer   notes

name

address · phone · website

opening hours

beers served / sold

my favourite beer

notes

name

address · phone · website

opening hours

beers served / sold

my favourite beer

notes

name

address · phone · website

opening hours

beers served / sold

my favourite beer

notes

name

address · phone · website   opening hours

beers served / sold

my favourite beer   notes

name

address · phone · website   opening hours

beers served / sold

my favourite beer   notes

name

address · phone · website   opening hours

beers served / sold

my favourite beer   notes

name

address · phone · website   opening hours

beers served / sold

my favourite beer   .   notes

name

address · phone · website   opening hours

beers served / sold

my favourite beer   notes

name

address · phone · website   opening hours

beers served / sold

my favourite beer   notes

beer

style

○ E+G
○ AG
○ ...

brewing date   bottling date

% alcohol   bitterness   colour   gravity

ABV   IBU   SRM   SG   OG   FG

grains · ingredients

hops

yeast   priming

mashing   boiling

notes

rating ☆☆☆☆☆

beer

style

- E+G
- AG
- ...

brewing date   bottling date

% alcohol	bitterness	colour	gravity		
ABV	IBU	SRM	SG	OG	FG

grains · ingredients

hops

yeast

priming

mashing

boiling

notes

rating ☆☆☆☆☆

beer

style

○ E+G

brewing date

bottling date

○ AG

○ ...

% alcohol   bitterness   colour   gravity

ABV   IBU   SRM   SG   OG   FG

grains · ingredients

hops

yeast

priming

mashing

boiling

notes

rating ☆☆☆☆☆

beer

style

○ E+G
○ AG
○ ...

brewing date   bottling date

% alcohol   bitterness   colour   gravity

| ABV | IBU | SRM | SG | OG | FG |

grains · ingredients

hops

yeast

priming

mashing

boiling

notes

rating ☆☆☆☆☆

beer

style

○ E+G
○ AG
○ ...

brewing date

bottling date

% alcohol   bitterness   colour   gravity

ABV   IBU   SRM   SG   OG   FG

grains · ingredients

hops

yeast

priming

mashing

boiling

notes

rating ☆☆☆☆☆

beer

style

○ E+G brewing date bottling date

○ AG

○ ...

% alcohol bitterness colour gravity

ABV IBU SRM SG OG FG

grains · ingredients

hops

yeast priming

mashing boiling

notes

rating ☆☆☆☆☆

beer

style

○ E+G   **brewing date**   **bottling date**
○ AG
○ ...

% alcohol   **bitterness**   **colour**   **gravity**

ABV   IBU   SRM   SG   OG   FG

grains · ingredients

hops

yeast   priming

mashing   boiling

notes

rating ☆☆☆☆☆

beer

style

○ E+G

brewing date   bottling date

○ AG

○ ...

% alcohol   bitterness   colour   gravity

ABV   IBU   SRM   SG   OG   FG

grains · ingredients

hops

yeast   priming

mashing   boiling

notes

rating ☆☆☆☆☆

beer   style

○ E+G   brewing date   bottling date
○ AG
○ ...

% alcohol   bitterness   colour   gravity

ABV   IBU   SRM   SG   OG   FG

grains · ingredients

hops

yeast   priming

mashing   boiling

notes

rating ☆☆☆☆☆

beer

style

- ○ E+G
- ○ AG
- ○ ...

brewing date   bottling date

% alcohol	bitterness	colour	gravity		
ABV	IBU	SRM	SG	OG	FG

grains · ingredients

hops

yeast

priming

mashing

boiling

notes

rating ☆☆☆☆☆

beer

style

- ○ E+G
- ○ AG
- ○ ...

brewing date   bottling date

% alcohol   bitterness   colour   gravity

ABV   IBU   SRM   SG   OG   FG

grains · ingredients

hops

yeast   priming

mashing   boiling

notes

rating ☆☆☆☆☆

beer

style

- ○ E+G
- ○ AG
- ○ ...

brewing date   bottling date

% alcohol   bitterness   colour   gravity

ABV   IBU   SRM   SG   OG   FG

grains · ingredients

hops

yeast   priming

mashing   boiling

notes

rating ☆☆☆☆☆

beer

style

○ E+G

○ AG

○ ...

brewing date   bottling date

% alcohol	bitterness	colour	gravity		
ABV	IBU	SRM	SG	OG	FG

grains · ingredients

hops

yeast   priming

mashing   boiling

notes

rating ☆☆☆☆☆

beer

style

- ○ E+G
- ○ AG
- ○ ...

brewing date   bottling date

% alcohol   bitterness   colour   gravity

| ABV | IBU | SRM | SG | OG | FG |

grains · ingredients

hops

yeast   priming

mashing   boiling

notes

rating ☆☆☆☆☆

beer

style

○ E+G
○ AG
○ ...

brewing date

bottling date

% alcohol

bitterness

colour

gravity

ABV

IBU

SRM

SG

OG

FG

grains · ingredients

hops

yeast

priming

mashing

boiling

notes

rating ☆☆☆☆☆

beer

style

○ E+G
○ AG
○ ...

brewing date

bottling date

% alcohol | bitterness | colour | gravity

ABV | IBU | SRM | SG | OG | FG

grains · ingredients

hops

yeast

priming

mashing

boiling

notes

rating ☆☆☆☆☆

beer

style

- E+G
- AG
- ...

brewing date   bottling date

% alcohol   bitterness   colour   gravity

ABV   IBU   SRM   SG   OG   FG

grains · ingredients

hops

yeast   priming

mashing   boiling

notes

rating ☆☆☆☆☆

beer

style

○ E+G

brewing date

bottling date

○ AG

○ ...

% alcohol	bitterness	colour	gravity		
ABV	IBU	SRM	SG	OG	FG

grains · ingredients

hops

yeast

priming

mashing

boiling

notes

rating ☆☆☆☆☆

beer   style

○ E+G   brewing date   bottling date
○ AG
○ ...

% alcohol   bitterness   colour   gravity

ABV   IBU   SRM   SG   OG   FG

grains · ingredients

hops

yeast   priming

mashing   boiling

notes

rating ☆☆☆☆☆

beer

style

- ○ E+G
- ○ AG
- ○ ...

brewing date   bottling date

% alcohol   bitterness   colour   gravity

ABV	IBU	SRM	SG	OG	FG

grains · ingredients

hops

yeast   priming

mashing   boiling

notes

rating ☆☆☆☆☆

beer   style

○ E+G   brewing date   bottling date
○ AG
○ ...

% alcohol   bitterness   colour   gravity

ABV   IBU   SRM   SG   OG   FG

grains · ingredients

hops

yeast   priming

mashing   boiling

notes

rating ☆☆☆☆☆

beer

style

○ E+G

brewing date

bottling date

○ AG

○ ...

% alcohol   bitterness   colour   gravity

ABV   IBU   SRM   SG   OG   FG

grains · ingredients

hops

yeast

priming

mashing

boiling

notes

rating ☆☆☆☆☆

beer

style

○ E+G

brewing date

bottling date

○ AG

○ ...

% alcohol

bitterness

colour

gravity

ABV

IBU

SRM

SG

OG

FG

grains · ingredients

hops

yeast

priming

mashing

boiling

notes

rating ☆☆☆☆☆

beer

style

- E+G
- AG
- ...

brewing date   bottling date

% alcohol   bitterness   colour   gravity

ABV	IBU	SRM	SG	OG	FG

grains · ingredients

hops

yeast

priming

mashing

boiling

notes

rating ☆☆☆☆☆

beer   style

○ E+G   brewing date   bottling date
○ AG
○ ...

% alcohol   bitterness   colour   gravity

ABV   IBU   SRM   SG   OG   FG

grains · ingredients

hops

yeast   priming

mashing   boiling

notes

rating ☆☆☆☆☆

beer

style

○ E+G   brewing date   bottling date
○ AG
○ …

% alcohol   bitterness   colour   gravity

ABV   IBU   SRM   SG   OG   FG

grains · ingredients

hops

yeast   priming

mashing   boiling

notes

rating ☆☆☆☆☆

beer

style

○ E+G
○ AG
○ ...

brewing date

bottling date

% alcohol | bitterness | colour | gravity

ABV | IBU | SRM | SG | OG | FG

grains · ingredients

hops

yeast

priming

mashing

boiling

notes

rating ☆☆☆☆☆

beer

style

- E+G
- AG
- ...

brewing date   bottling date

% alcohol	bitterness	colour	gravity		
ABV	IBU	SRM	SG	OG	FG

grains · ingredients

hops

yeast

priming

mashing

boiling

notes

rating ☆☆☆☆☆

beer   style

○ E+G   brewing date   bottling date
○ AG
○ ...

% alcohol   bitterness   colour   gravity

ABV   IBU   SRM   SG   OG   FG

grains · ingredients

hops

yeast   priming

mashing   boiling

notes

rating ☆☆☆☆☆

beer

style

- ○ E+G
- ○ AG
- ○ ...

brewing date

bottling date

% alcohol	bitterness	colour	gravity		
ABV	IBU	SRM	SG	OG	FG

grains · ingredients

hops

yeast

priming

mashing

boiling

notes

rating ☆☆☆☆☆

Index

146

147

148

149

150

151

152

153

154

155

156

157

158

159

160

161

162

163

164

165

166

Ruled Pages 167

168

169

170

171

172

173

174

175

176

177

178

179

180

181

182

183

184

185

186

187

188

189

190

Divided Pages 191

192

193